THE
DUMBING
DOWN OF
BRITAIN

THE DUMBING DOWN OF BRITAIN

DUNCAN BARKES

LEADING BRITAIN'S CONVERSATION
DAB DIGITAL RADIO | 97.3 FM

&

First published 2015 by
Elliott and Thompson Limited
27 John Street
London WC1N 2BX
www.eandtbooks.com

ISBN: 978-1-78396-094-1

A catalogue record for this book is available from the
British Library.

Managing Editor, LBC: James Rea
Deputy Managing Editor, LBC: Tom Cheal

Typesetting: Marie Doherty
Printed in the UK by TJ International Ltd

Contents

Introduction

Among my friends and colleagues this book became fondly referred to as 'Angry Words' while it was being written. There are quite a few of them in here, but I hope they are more than just the misanthropic rants from a man hurtling into middle age in a slightly bewildered fashion.

Britain has become a more dumbed-down nation than ever before and this book will hopefully give you an insight as to why I feel this is the situation we currently find ourselves in. I hope you enjoy it.

And please let me take this opportunity to thank you if you are a regular listener to my LBC shows. Sometimes they can be robust, thought-provoking, insightful, bloody and downright frustrating but, let's face it — the world would be a very dull place if we simply agreed all the time. One thing is for sure: my radio shows would be nothing without my listeners. Thank you for playing a vital part.

1
Not voting

One of the traits of our dumbed-down society is the fact that people do not bother to vote any more. There has been a gradual decline in those turning out to vote in elections over recent decades. Politicians and academics spend many hours trying to work out why and ponder how best to get people to use their vote. The right to vote is a privilege — it is valuable and there are people around the world prepared to die for the simple right to have it. In Britain we treat it with contempt and act as if it is a chore to use it — this stinking attitude needs to change.

The fudge I often hear includes: 'politicians are all the same', 'my vote won't make any difference', 'politics has nothing to do with me' and 'it's my right not to vote'. Let's take each of these lame excuses and pick them apart. It won't take long.

Politicians are not 'all the same'. Of course the expenses scandal left a whiffy cloud lingering over Westminster and the electorate are right to remain suspicious. We trusted our MPs to use their allowances in a fair and honourable way and some abused that trust, but it does not automatically follow that they are all in it for the money or self-interest.

To suggest that all MPs are the same is akin to saying that all teachers sleep with their pupils and every football fan is a thug. It is lazy thinking used by many to justify their reasons for not going to the ballot box. There are hundreds of decent, hardworking and honest MPs who want to do their best for the country.

The deceased union leader Bob Crow was once quoted as saying: 'Spit on your own and you can't do anything, but if you all spit together you can drown the bastards.' Bob, of course, was the General Secretary of the National Union of Rail, Maritime and Transport Workers and was often roundly criticised for causing the London Underground to grind to a halt when his union's members voted for strike action.

Regardless of your political standpoint, his words make absolute sense. The idea that your vote will not make any difference is folly and again is a line used all too often by those looking for a convenient excuse. Your vote *does* count, it *can* make a difference.

Two examples spring to mind. In 2001, Richard Taylor stood as an independent parliamentary candidate in Wyre Forest. He was not a typical career politician — he was a doctor who campaigned on the single issue of restoring the Accident and Emergency department at Kidderminster Hospital. The facility had been closed in 2000 due to NHS cuts. Taylor won the election with a whopping majority of around 18,000, beating the incumbent Labour MP. Taylor remained MP for the constituency until 2010.

Martin Bell was the former BBC war reporter who stood as an independent candidate in the Tatton constituency in Cheshire in 1997. The MP at the time was the Conservative minister Neil Hamilton, who was the subject of allegations regarding 'sleaze'. Bell stood on an 'anti-sleaze' platform and won. He overturned a Conservative majority of around 22,000 and became the first successful independent parliamentary candidate since 1951.

One could argue that both these cases partly owe their success to the political mischief of rival parties who were keen to bloody the nose of the incumbent MPs, but it does prove that your vote can count and make a significant difference.

Politics is everywhere. The idea that it does not affect you or has nothing to do with your life is remarkably short-sighted or, perhaps, the view of someone who is a bit dim. It affects each and every one of us. Politics determines the amount of tax we pay, the standard of care we receive from the NHS, how good our children's education is, the currency we use, and whether or not there are enough houses to live in and jobs to do. And if none of that matters to you, then politics is ultimately responsible for how often your bins get emptied.

Perhaps the worst excuse people give for not voting is that it is their right not to. This view is normally articulated with sneering disgust that someone dare suggest that an individual actually stop complaining and do something positive about their frustrations. If you do not vote, then as far as I am concerned, you have no right to complain.

And rights are the key here. There are still many countries around the world where whole populations do not have the right to vote. They desperately crave democracy but their rulers or dictators refuse to give it. Those that dare speak up or protest for the simple right to vote can often find themselves and their families persecuted.

Right now there are people being kept in horrendous conditions and being tortured because all they want is the right to vote. The contrast is vast: some poor soul is having electrodes attached to their most sensitive parts and being beaten within an inch of their life because they want democracy, while in Britain we have vast chunks of the population that bleat about it being their right not to vote. Perhaps they should swap places?

There *is* a disconnection between politicians and the electorate, but it is not just down to the political class to change this. It is a two-way street and we all have a part to play.

At the last election, the Electoral Commission worked out there were six million voters missing from the electoral register. These are people that live in Britain who have not even bothered to register to vote. This is on top of the many millions who have registered, but simply choose not to bother to go to the ballot box.

It should be clear to you by now that I see this country's growing cancer of apathy as an indication of a depressing shift in society that sees many more engaged in and concerned about voting in some naff TV talent show than who runs their country.

And if you think I am making this up, then ponder this: a poll by *Cosmopolitan* magazine of eighteen- to thirty-year-old women in 2014 found that 3 per cent said they would vote for reality-TV star Joey Essex. Bear in mind this is the man who, on national TV, was actually proud of the fact he needed someone to help him tell the time.

Perhaps the time has come to adopt the Australian approach to voting and make it compulsory. This system sees the individual having to register, attend a polling station and have their name ticked off to show they have turned up and a ballot paper has been put in a box — failure to do this will result in a fine.

There is also an argument to say that it should be made easier to vote. In an age of modern technology it cannot be beyond the wit of man to devise a secure and robust method that would allow the electorate to vote using text messaging or the Internet. As the younger generations seem to have a panic attack when parted from their mobile phones for more than ten minutes, it would be a wise government that developed such a system.

The lack of interest and engagement in politics is a travesty — the same old lame excuses given for not voting simply do not stand up to scrutiny. In many cases our apathetic Britain has only got itself to blame for the state it finds itself in. But is it any wonder when nowadays many people are unable or unwilling to communicate verbally with their fellow human beings?

2
We don't talk any more

Today's Britain has been partly created by the march of technology. The great leaps forward made possible due to new inventions should be progress that is widely celebrated; instead it seems to be having a detrimental effect on society when it comes to how we communicate.

We now seem to be living in a country where basic human interaction is shunned as the microchip has taken over. I am aware that I am in danger of sounding like a Luddite — one of those nineteenth-century textile artisans who protested against labour-saving machinery such as power looms and spinning frames during the Industrial Revolution.

I have no issue with technology that makes a job easier — my gripe is that it has reduced people's brains to mush as they rely on email, the Internet, Facebook, Twitter and text as a way of communicating and receiving information.

Text-speak has seen our beautiful language reduced to a strange mix of letters and numbers in order to create words. Gr8, you might think, but when teachers report that text-speak is finding its way into how pupils write their work, you have to concede that we have a bit of a problem (and that's before you start to address the worrying views of various 'academic experts' who defend its use as they believe it does not matter how a pupil communicates or how much they have bastardised the English language).

The mobile phone may have made many people's lives simpler, but it has also made us lazy. Instead of finding the time to actually talk with somebody, many communicate by sending misspelled messages that, at a stroke, kill the art of conversation.

You would think that a camera on a mobile phone would see people capturing those magical moments and then remembering those good times when they have a moment to themselves, but no. Cameras on phones have resulted in an explosion of the kind of self-obsessed behaviour that really requires therapy. From the ghastly pastime of 'selfies', to taking a picture of that day's breakfast and sharing it on social media, a great invention has become abused to generate self-absorbed twaddle.

The explosion of social media has fuelled

revolutions over recent years and has certainly seen oppressed people gaining access to information and a form of communication that previously they had never dreamed was possible. Facebook and Twitter have also allowed far-flung friends to re-establish contact and for users to utilise both platforms to raise millions of pounds for charity. The case of cancer sufferer Stephen Sutton was a prime example.

However, the majority of social media these days is no more than a modern-day version of being invited to someone else's house to view their rather tedious holiday snaps. I use Twitter for my radio shows and to gather opinions for any articles I might be working on, but if I was not in this line of work, I would be off it in a shot.

These days it seems everyone using social media is living their life through it. Someone buys a new car or books a holiday and cannot wait to tell their social media followers. Their pet dog looks vaguely cute having a nap so they share a picture with the rest of the world. Such behaviour is the worst kind of navel-gazing.

One of the most despicable symptoms of our social media-obsessed society is the outpouring of grief that it encourages users to demonstrate. Of course a death is a cruel and life-shattering experience for close friends and family, but what happened to grief being an intensely private emotion? What's worse is when social media mobilises people to grieve over the demise of a person that they never knew or even met.

The power of social media should not be underestimated though. Upset some of its most prolific users, such as Stephen Fry or Caitlin Moran, and it is akin to Krakatoa erupting as their millions of Twitter followers light their cyber-burning torches and an online witch hunt begins.

Twitter, in particular, has also given an outlet to the worst kind of person who hides behind their computer keyboard and abuses, harasses, threatens and intimidates others. Someone once said that Twitter is the last refuge of the green-ink brigade, and they are absolutely right.

Texting and the growth of social media is not only killing off conversation, but it is turning the nation into a society that views the world through a small screen.

The Internet is an amazing invention, but it has also had a negative impact on how we live our lives. Shopping online is killing the high street and encourages transactions without any human interaction. And because the Internet remains, rightly, unregulated, it has become a tool for some to spread misinformation. Online forums, for example, sometimes contains information based on hearsay, but repeated often enough across the web, people start to use such information as 'facts'. We are creating a generation that believes everything it reads online and this is highly dangerous.

My heart goes out to a retired art teacher called Anne who ended her life at the Dignitas clinic in Switzerland in early 2014. Anne was not terminally ill or seriously disabled — she made the decision to commit suicide because she was frustrated at the lack of interaction in modern life and our reliance on computers and the Internet. She told the *Sunday Times*: 'People are becoming more and more remote. We are becoming robots. It is this lack of humanity.'

When I read Anne's story, I was struck by how isolating it must be to live in a world which is increasingly geared around an online and texting generation, where the art of conversation in real time is sadly becoming marginalised.

It is not just social media and mobiles — the technology used when buying goods and services has replaced jobs and left the consumer with a substandard service. Two notable examples are the increase in automated phone systems when all you really want to do is talk to a human being because none of the 'options' you are offered by the cyber-voice fit your enquiry; and the unstoppable rise of those self-service tills in supermarkets.

From a business perspective, both are a big step forward as they reduce costs and free up resources; from a customer service viewpoint they raise the blood pressure and make you feel undervalued as a person who only wants to spend your hard-earned money. Give it a few decades and someone will come up with the radical idea of human beings actually talking with customers and they will be hailed as some kind of retail genius.

I am not anti-technology, but I see all too easily how it is creating a generation that does not possess the very basics when it comes to written and oral communication.

Talk to anyone involved in recruiting and employment — they will tell you that when it comes to interviews there are applicants in their twenties and thirties who cannot hold a conversation and are socially inept. This is partly due to a reliance on technology that has removed these basic life skills.

Technological advances should be embraced if they make the world a better place and improve the quality of life, but I fear that when it comes to communication, technology has taken us backwards. Attempt a conversation with some people these days and you would get more sense from a chimp banging a set of drums. And, of course, the less we communicate effectively about the stuff that really matters, such as freedom, liberty and democracy, the easier it is for governments to do what they want, such as ban smoking.

3
You can't smoke here

It was a dark day in 2007 when the smoking ban was introduced. This illiberal piece of legislation appears to have done little to help people quit smoking so one wonders what the real purpose was, apart from to create a society that happily allows the state to tell them how to live their lives. If we weren't so dumb, perhaps we would do more about this stripping away of our liberty.

Britain has a vicious anti-smoking lobby and it was this screeching minority that ensured the ban came into force. I remain convinced that those politicians, charities and medical professionals who seem hell-bent on stubbing out smoking will not be happy until the last packet of Marlboro disappears from these shores.

I have not smoked cigarettes for over twenty years, but I will go in to bat for anyone who does, as the opposition to consuming this perfectly legal product is way off the scale. Fags make people smell, muck up your teeth and can kill you — but while they remain legitimately on sale in this country, the persecution of smokers has to stop. Smokers are treated like lepers in today's society, which is perverse as the government makes a fortune out of them in tax.

The night before the smoking ban was implemented in Britain, I enjoyed several courses, many glasses, and various cigars of distinction at The Last Indoor Cigar Party at a hotel in Brighton. It seemed fitting to mourn the passing of freedom in such decadent surroundings. Around one hundred people from all walks of life had gathered to mourn the loss of freedom and liberty. The central topic of conversation was based around one word: compromise.

Smokers accept that their habit is not to everyone's taste and most would never dream of intentionally inflicting second-hand smoke on anyone. But an outright ban on puffing away in a public place seems extreme.

The compromise solution still exists. Allow venues to be smoking or non-smoking. Pubs could have a ventilated smoking room where non-smokers would not need to go. Consumers would decide where they would happily drink and dine and we will finally see the long overdue return of freedom of choice. In other words, let the market decide. In a town which had a venue with a smoking room, and one that did not, my bet is that both businesses would prosper.

But in the absence of some enlightened thinking, let's look at what the smoking ban has achieved. Figures released by the National Office of Statistics in 2013 revealed that despite the introduction of the ban in 2007, the number of people smoking in Britain has remained the same. One of the key arguments behind this draconian piece of legislation was that it would mean people giving up smoking — clearly that has not been the case.

We do know that the ban has played a part in decimating the pub trade, with thousands of pubs across the country closing for good. It has also contributed to tens of thousands of jobs being lost in the leisure industry as not only pubs closed, but also clubs and bingo halls.

Does this matter? Of course it does. While the impact of the ban may seem minimal inside the M25, a trip outside of greater London to the north of England has seen venues at the heart of their communities close for good.

If you think this is perhaps a tad over-emotional, then consider this: the Trimdon Constituency Labour Club, the Sedgefield working men's bar made famous by Tony Blair in his constituency after he announced there he would stand for election as Labour leader, closed on 21 July 2010, citing the smoking ban as one of the key reasons for shutting up shop. How utterly perverse — a ban brought in under Blair's New Labour government ended up closing down a place where many of its customers had voted for their local MP and supported his campaign to become prime minister.

Those who still support the smoking ban will invariably highlight the positive impact on the health of those working in the venues that still remain open, but it is really not that clear-cut.

A report by the Scientific Committee on Tobacco and Health showed that the increased risk of lung cancer from second-hand cigarette smoke was 24 per cent, but this figure is low compared to other risks faced by workers.

According to Cancer Research UK, the increased risk of contracting lung cancer if you work in a profession that regularly exposes you to diesel fumes is 47 per cent. Outside of the workplace, a French study suggested that a typical garden barbecue releases the same number of dioxins that would be emitted from 220,000 cigarettes.

Where are the campaigns to ban diesel engines or to stop people cooking steaks over coals in their back gardens? The health argument is a weak one when you look at these statistics, but I believe the continued targeting of smokers is not just about the health of the nation — it is about control and those that shout the loudest.

I accept that smoking is not good for you, but neither is drinking, eating fast food or not taking enough exercise. Encourage healthy choices by all means, but banning things is the behaviour of extremists.

Smokers get the rough end of the stick. We frequently hear of 'binge-drinking Britain' when it comes to alcohol and you cannot escape the looming obesity crisis. In both cases we are lectured about the negative impact on our health and the burden that will be placed on the NHS if we do not cut down the booze or lose a few stone. The same arguments are used when preaching about the evils of smoking, but it is far from a level playing field.

Go into any supermarket these days to purchase tobacco and sometimes it seems it might be easier to score dope on the high street. All products are hidden out of sight behind metal shutters in a move that would not be out of place in the Prohibition era. Yet fatty foods or products with a high sugar content are openly on display and bottles of alcohol are there for all to see. Surely the same restrictions should apply to these health-damaging products too?

The same disparity exists with the ongoing tedious debate about cigarettes in plain packaging. If such a measure really stops or discourages people from smoking, then presumably wine and beer should be marketed in plain bottles and cans. Again, using this flawed logic, biscuits and doughnuts should also be sold in bleak and unidentifiable packaging to stop people scoffing them.

Smokers are unfairly targeted by politicians and health professionals in Britain. The smoking ban in public or enclosed spaces was just the beginning. A few years ago one local councillor in the market town of Stony Stratford in Buckinghamshire tried to introduce an even more extreme law.

He proposed that smoking be banned in parks, streets and any public space. If caught, a smoker would be issued with a fixed penalty notice by a Police Community Support Officer. Thankfully, saner minds prevailed and he had little support among his fellow councillors.

However, we do know that there are plans to ban smoking in cars that are carrying children, which is also a further step towards eroding individual freedom. No smoker I know would dream of puffing away with a child in the car, but it will soon be against the law, though one wonders how it can ever be effectively policed.

The most sinister element of this new law is that if you agree with the principle that people should be told by the state how to behave in their own space, i.e. their car, then surely it is only a short step away from telling people that they cannot smoke in their own homes. Sadly, I think that day is not too far away.

There are roughly ten million smokers in Britain, most of whom pay vast amounts of tax to enjoy a perfectly legal product, yet they are treated like pariahs. I used to think that the British sense of fair play would prevail and this persecution of smokers would eventually stop, but I actually think it has just started. The introduction of the smoking ban was a grim day for a country which used to have a reputation for fairness, tolerance and compromise. To accept this form of state intervention and follow it like sheep demonstrates a worrying decline in our acceptance of personal responsibility. This

growing lack of interest in making our own decisions is leading to a level of ignorance that is
becoming ever more apparent in many areas of
life; for example, knowing where the food we put
in our mouths comes from and how it is created.

4

Do fish fingers come from a pig?

Many people don't have a clue where the food on their plate comes from. Isn't it ironic that the medical profession is constantly warning us about this country's looming obesity crisis and the growing number of people waddling around the streets, yet knowledge about food is increasingly scant? We are getting fatter, but many are simply ignorant about the food they are stuffing in their gobs.

The demise of the high street has gone hand in hand with the explosion of supermarkets across the country. Some of you reading this will recall a time where your local high street had a greengrocer, a butcher, a baker and, if you were lucky, a fishmonger. Unless you were a little bit dim, it was clear where the food had come from.

Shop window displays featuring hanging carcasses or the head of a dead pig left us in no doubt that your beef or pork came from a cow or a pig. A fishmonger might have whole piles of mackerel on display, or crabs and lobster. There was an immediate, visual understanding of what the food was and where it came from. These days, in a climate where most of the nation shop at their local supermarket, a disconnection has developed between where the food comes from and what ends up in a neatly wrapped polystyrene and plastic package.

If you think this is an extreme assessment when it comes to the appalling lack of food knowledge that exists today, consider the following.

The British Nutrition Foundation recently found that a quarter of primary school children believe that fish fingers come from chicken or pigs. It is disgraceful that many children have no understanding of the origins of what's on their dinner plate.

You would have thought the word 'fish' would have provided a stonking clue, but no: one in four still think they come from something with feathers or a snout.

I used to take the view that certain things in life should be taught to children by their parents and it should not be the job of the state, but it is now clear that parents cannot always be relied upon. We either have mums and dads serving up food to their kids without troubling to explain what it is or where it came from, or else — more alarmingly — they do not know themselves.

Our attitude to food and being honest about where it comes from is, frankly, embarrassing. You may have seen those River Cottage television programmes presented by the chef and campaigner Hugh Fearnley-Whittingstall. As well as trying to get us to eat more veg, Hugh also tries to educate folk about food.

One particular programme featured a lady with a rather excessive habit of buying buckets of fried chicken. Hugh got her to look after the chickens on his farm and, of course, she was mortified when he told her that the chicken she had become attached to would have to be killed for her dinner. She was in bits.

It really does make you wonder where some people think the food on their plate comes from. I take the rather more robust view that will win me few friends, but if you are not prepared to kill an animal yourself, then perhaps you should be considering whether or not it is right for you to eat it.

Society's increasingly warped attitude to food reached a new low in 2014 when a market butcher was forced to remove displays of raw meat from its window because it upset passers-by. JBS Family Butchers in the market town of Sudbury in Suffolk has been in business for over one hundred years. Their window displays were a sight to behold — hanging pheasants, rabbits and partridges, along with the occasional head of a pig or deer.

But a vicious campaign ensued from those who had moved to the area and were unhappy with the display. They wrote to the local newspaper complaining, sent hate mail to the business and took to Facebook to try to create a boycott of the shop.

One critic told the local newspaper: 'As someone who breeds rabbits, I find the display of animals hanging in the window disgusting. It has continental giant rabbits, pigs' heads and ducks. It must be upsetting for children who have animals.'

Another complained that the 'needless display of multiple mutilated carcasses' had stopped him taking his twelve-year-old daughter to the nearby sweetshop. The angry parent went on: 'We avoid the entire precinct as we'd rather not look at bloody severed pigs' heads when buying sweets. I am asking for JBS to be more considerate with what they display in their window.'

Is it any wonder, with parents like this bringing up children, that we have kids in this country that believe fish fingers come from pigs? Thankfully, despite this vitriolic campaign and initially removing their display, the butcher returned to form after receiving significant support from loyal customers. But the mindset of those that complained, sadly, speaks volumes.

Some schools make a decent attempt at trying to educate pupils about where their food comes from, but it does not always go according to plan.

Let me tell you the story of Marcus, a lamb raised by pupils at a school in Kent. As part of a rather brilliant project designed to teach children about the origins of food, he was raised and then slaughtered, with the meat featuring as the star prize in the school raffle.

Parents were outraged, some claiming that their children were traumatised. Others threatened legal action. Following threats of attacking the school from some locals, the police got involved. I bet many of those who made threats still enjoy roast lamb on a Sunday. The whiff of hypocrisy from those who get all squeamish over where their food comes from and animal slaughter is pretty potent at times.

And if we are ever to combat the rising obesity crisis, then robust food education is vital. If kids don't know that burgers come from cows, then they are unlikely to be aware of trans-fats, empty calories and the poor nutritional value of most processed foods.

I would stop short of suggesting that every child should be taken on a visit to an abattoir, but a trip to a farm accompanied by a narrative detailing the journey from pasture to slaughter-house would leave children in no doubt as to the origin of the bacon in their butties.

Our attitude to food can be summed up by a product that was launched by a certain pizza restaurant chain a while back: The Cheeseburger Pizza Crust. Their website said it all: 'When eating out, there is always a choice — burger or pizza? Now you don't have to make that choice!' I am not sure if the word 'pizza' should really have been used to describe that creation. It looked liked the creation of a chef with ADHD on a bad acid trip.

Presumably the company carried out market research before launching the product and must have received the thumbs up from potential customers. That people actually like the idea of pizza somehow combined with burgers makes me think that the taste buds of these would-be munchers should be forcibly removed and given to those who actually appreciate food. Food — not chemically enhanced and processed fat.

It's not a pizza. Wander into a restaurant in Italy and you will find proper cooks making dough, producing a thin base and adding a simple topping of fresh ingredients. That's a pizza. Adding a cheeseburger crust is simply satisfying the gluttonous demands of obese Britons who would not know a decent dish if it smacked them in the chops.

We live in a country where, increasingly, the cosmetic is all that matters. People spend fortunes on everything from gym memberships to fashionable clothes, make-up to Botox, but seem ignorant of what they are actually putting into their bodies.

Instead they live off ready meals, unable or unwilling to cook anything decent, but then become hypersensitive and offended over anything that goes some way to explaining or showing where the chicken on their plate or the beef in their bun comes from. The ignorance of the origins of food, the animals that provide it and how it is created gives you a real flavour of how dumbed down our society has become.

However, this should come as no surprise as all so many people seem to care about these days is instant gratification — and, boy, they certainly get agitated over anything they feel (selfishly) will interfere with their interests and lifestyles.

5
The rise of the NIMBY

Folk may not know or care what's in their ready meal, but they will be the first to man the barricades to oppose developments that would benefit Britain for decades to come. The rise of the NIMBY has much to do with the sorry state that we find ourselves in and they certainly seem to be shouting the loudest over all kinds of matters.

NIMBY, of course, is an acronym for Not In My Back Yard and it is fast becoming a national sport for many. A local council or the government might dare to float an idea that could improve services in an area, provide more housing or boost the national infrastructure and, rest assured, outrage and indignation is never too far behind from those who oppose progress.

Nowadays it is so easy to mount opposition that it is hard not to conclude that some people would have nothing left in their lives if they had nothing to moan about. A few mouse clicks on a computer, some emotive and knee-jerk-fuelled words and you instantly have a campaign website.

Add to the mix an online petition that requires little effort to set up or, indeed, sign and a Facebook group that people can 'like' from the comfort of their own armchair while watching *Coronation Street*, and you have a ready-made campaign up and running to oppose whatever takes your fancy.

This insular and selfish form of behaviour is causing this country to stand still. As we become so obsessed with 'now' and many seem to lack the foresight to think about the future, we end up going nowhere, apart from round and round in ever-decreasing circles where nothing gets done.

The NIMBY naturally opposes anything that affects them personally — they are motivated only by self-interest and, unless robustly challenged, their attitude will see Britain lagging behind while other nations grow and prosper.

Examples of the NIMBY at work are rife. Take the long-running saga regarding High Speed 2 (HS2), the new rail network being proposed to link London with the Midlands and the north of England.

It is an emotive issue when you consider that some parts of the glorious Chilterns will be ploughed up in order to build the rail link. This is when NIMBY Britain really gets on its moral high horse; when it feels that our ample green and pleasant land is under threat.

Of course HS2 means some greenbelt land will be utilised and some properties bulldozed, but unless this happens we will be left with a decrepit rail system which will soon be unfit for purpose. Many critics seem unable to grasp this basic fact and instead bleat on about the cost or the damage to some parts of the countryside.

Our existing rail system is fast becoming junked — try travelling on it at the weekend and witness the vast amount of engineering works that take place just to keep it functioning as it is. We desperately need new lines and tracks and should be embracing new technology, not opposing it.

Failure to think sensibly about our future transport needs will see Britain become a laughing stock compared to countries such as China, where they understand the importance and value of continually upgrading and developing their rail networks. This country's inability to view things in the long term will surely be our undoing.

Airport capacity is another area where short-term thinking and rampant NIMBYism will see Britain left behind. Various politicians have staked their careers on opposing a third runway at Heathrow Airport. Successive governments have kicked the issue of airport expansion into the long grass, but it has now reached a critical stage.

We are in danger of airlines deciding to base their operations in other European cities, so it is vital that we seriously address the need for more capacity and better facilities. If we want to continue to capitalise on London as a tourist destination and enjoy the wealth that this brings to the nation when people visit, and if we are serious about being a country that is a business capital of the world, then we need to be investing in and improving our airports.

Instead, wherever you look there is staunch opposition to any of the possible suggestions. Residents near Heathrow airport have made it very clear they do not want a third runway. A coalition of green campaigners, celebrities, politicians and scientists have already purchased land earmarked for the construction of a third runway in the area, which has to be the ultimate sign of diva behaviour. A handful of C-list names stand in the way of Britain's future economic growth — it's the NIMBY in the worst possible light.

Similar opposition exists to the expansion of Gatwick, which, by my reckoning, is the most sensible option of all, yet you know that when a government finally finds the balls to make a decision about how we are going to increase airport capacity in Britain there will be protest groups and the usual suspects lying in front of bulldozers and hurling abuse at police officers.

Greenbelt land features heavily in the mind of the NIMBY and housing development is an obvious bone of contention, especially in many parts of south-east England.

Property prices are expensive and there is a clear shortage of houses. Many youngsters leaving home are forced to look to different parts of the country if they want to gain a footing on the properly ladder in terms of ownership. In some parts of Britain even renting a home is becoming a financial challenge. For many people in their thirties and forties, the idea of owning a property is becoming a distant dream. If you live in greater London, Kent, Essex, Hampshire, Surrey, Sussex, Buckinghamshire or Oxfordshire, affording your own home is becoming one of the biggest challenges you will face in life.

The obvious solution is to build more housing, but nobody wants it near them. I have lost count of the number of campaigns I have come across where residents are opposed to a nearby housing development. I accept this has to go hand in hand with an investment in infrastructure, but simply saying a big fat 'NO' to more houses is essentially selfish and inward-looking. It is also letting down future generations who, in some parts of the country, will simply never be able to afford a home of their own.

The latest issue that has seriously galvanised the NIMBY is fracking — the process of injecting liquid at high pressure in subterranean rocks, which forces open existing fissures in order to extract oil or gas.

It is an issue so riddled with knee-jerk rhetoric and misinformation that it is difficult to know where to start, but that does not stop the NIMBY at the height of their powers. They latch on to the scare stories, do little proper research themselves and dig in to oppose something that would not only mean cheaper energy bills for those already struggling to make ends meet, but would provide a significant economic boost to the country, as we have seen in the USA.

NIMBIES won't even flirt with the idea and proper informed debate about this topic is almost impossible; all attempts at sensible dialogue are drowned out by the shrieking of campaigners with nothing but self-interest at heart, occasionally dressed up as concerns about the environment.

It is worth remembering that we have a track record in Britain when it comes to standing in the way of progress. A trawl through the archives will show significant opposition in the past to projects such as the M25 or the Channel Tunnel, but, ultimately, these initiatives were pushed forwards for the good of the country.

Many people in Britain seem to have lost the intellectual ability to think further ahead or seem unable to put their own self-interest to one side for the future development and prosperity of the nation. Their thinking seems remarkably short-termist and shows no regard for how we should be investing in this country in such a way that it continues to be world class in decades to come.

The NIMBY is a barrier to progress and Britain is in serious danger of being left behind. Attitudes need to change before we shudder to a complete halt. There was a time when this could be achieved through good old-fashioned debate and argument, but not any more.

6
I am entitled
to my opinion

Britain has lost its ability to debate. I am not sure when the rot set in, but we now exist in a society where if you dare to offer an alternative point of view or if you deviate from what is perceived as the right position to hold, there can be hell to pay.

Perhaps I see it more than most because I present a nightly radio phone-in, but it is everywhere. Even in my limited time inhabiting radio studios, there has been a noticeable decline over the last twenty years in the ability to debate a particular issue.

No one is suggesting that everybody should be graduating from some Oxbridge debating society with the skills to influence and persuade an audience, but a little bit of thinking before blurting out the latest tabloid headline or cliché would be most welcome.

Phone-in radio works in a certain way. You pick a topic that you know the audience are interested in and will react to. And, because phone-in radio is based around interaction, you then take a stance on a certain issue or out-line possible opinions that may be held given whatever is being discussed. You then watch the switchboard to see how the audience reacts.

I love phone-in radio as it offers a snapshot of what people think and feel on any given subject. I would rather talk to a series of callers and try to understand their thinking than a dull politician with a carefully crafted script.

The problem arises when you start asking callers about their opinion. Many simply cannot explain why they hold it or how they have reached a certain conclusion. There is no right or wrong as far as I am concerned, but if you cannot articulate why you have a certain view, should you be phoning up a radio station and telling people all about it? The stock-phrase 'I am entitled to my opinion' is often rolled out as soon as a challenging question is asked. But are you really entitled to an opinion if you do not know how you got it? I think not.

Too many people hear someone else's view and repeat it or swallow a newspaper headline and quote it verbatim, yet really do not know what they think about it. And this kills debate. A robust exchange of views is delicious and can be a beautiful thing, but it appears to be dying out.

The art of thinking through a position and arguing it convincingly is increasingly rare. These days it descends into personal abuse all too quickly with critics playing the man and not the ball. Mind you, as this tactic is often used in Prime Minister's Questions, is it any wonder that others follow suit?

It is depressing that many do not seem to know why they think what they do, but a greater concern is the vitriol used to slap down an opposing viewpoint. This seems particularly rife in the charity sector, where criticism is simply banned. Here are two examples that demonstrate this well.

Henry Marsh is a neurosurgeon at a hospital in London. He made a remark about how useless cycle helmets were and said that they were flimsy and offered no protection. As a cyclist himself he does not wear one and he explained, as a neurosurgeon, that he had operated on many patients who had been in bike accidents and the helmet had not helped them one bit.

You could almost hear the collective sharp intakes of breath from Britain's self-appointed safety militants a mile off, the sound of their tut-tutting enough to cause a tremor.

Within hours the various charities, including the Bicycle Helmet Trust Initiative, rounded on Mr Marsh and gave him a good kicking. This charity wheeled out their chief executive, who said: 'I hope he is going to take responsibility for the cyclist who gets injured because they take their helmet off following his comments.'

Take a look at that quote and how knee-jerk it is. The neurosurgeon, a man who knows a hell of a lot more about what protects the brain than a chief executive of a special interest charity, offers a view which conflicts with the 'approved' position regarding cycle helmets. He is then effectively made complicit in any injuries that a cyclist may sustain because they decided not to wear a helmet following his comments.

This practice of automatic condemnation shuts down debate at a stroke and paints those with an opposing view as some kind of demon.

Behaviour like this is on the increase, and it is a tactic frequently used by those in the voluntary or campaigning sectors. Some of this country's most left-wing activists and journalists are also guilty of shutting down debate because they do not like the alternative viewpoint being offered.

I have personally encountered this tactic when I have questioned the growing spread of '20's Plenty' campaigns across Britain. For the uninitiated, this campaign calls for 20 mph speed limits on residential roads in towns and cities.

Such schemes already exist in Portsmouth and Bristol and some London boroughs, but there are dozens of campaign groups across the country who want the same in their part of Britain. Birmingham, Manchester, Crewe, Sunderland — the list is pretty endless. Yet search around for evidence that such schemes make much difference and it will take you a long time. The evidence bandied about by campaigners is, at best, flaky.

You have probably worked out by now that I do not like being told what to do. So when such a scheme was proposed where I live, I questioned its logic rigorously. My first encounter with local campaigners was in the playground of my daughter's school. As a dutiful parent I had turned up to support the school fete and was accosted by a couple of women standing behind a trestle table and proffering a petition to sign.

They explained that they were collecting signatures to force the local council to examine the idea of 20 mph speed limits on residential roads in the district and would I sign it as I clearly had a child and would care about her safety.

One simple question set them off on a rant of such indignant fury it was like daring to question the zealous views of some evil despot. I asked them where the evidence was that showed such a measure actually made the roads safer. They looked at me in such a way you would have thought I had asked them to strip and perform a lap dance.

I do not go out of my way to look for arguments, but I only sign petitions once I have explored the issue and made my own mind up. I just wish many more people would do the same.

My refusal to sign was followed up with a parting salvo that they hoped nothing terrible would happen to my daughter when using the local residential roads as a result of a speeding motorist. If I was living in Sicily I would have taken this as some kind of Mafia-style threat.

This is not about 'right' or 'wrong', it is all about participating in a robust exchange of views and an acceptance that others may hold a different opinion to yours. Sadly this ability is dying out, as is the capability to reasonably argue a point as opposed to resorting to gut reaction, rhetoric, abuse or threats.

Changes such as this in our fundamental behaviour and attitudes are beginning to show in many areas of life; one that strikes me in particular is the emergence of the so-called 'modern man'. While women rightly go from strength to strength as the fight against inequality continues, we have, over the last ten years, seen the emergence of a new kind of dumbed-down man — and it is not a pretty sight to behold.

7
Where have all the real men gone?

I am often ashamed to be a man these days. This is not because of my own behaviour, but because when I look around at what is increasingly representative of 'modern man', I feel embarrassed and ashamed by what I see.

Modern men are a bit of a joke. Armed with their 'man bags' and often spending more time in the bathroom than their partner, so-called metrosexuality has gone too far. Modern man also seems scared of having an opinion for fear of causing offence. Our forefathers would be spluttering into their dimpled pint glasses at the state of many of today's men, wondering where it all went wrong.

Nobody is suggesting a return to the days of the caveman or knuckle-dragging behaviour. I am not advocating that today's males start watching past episodes of *The Sweeney* and transform themselves into some kind of sexist monster, but I do think today's men need to find a bit of gumption.

I am not alone in my concerns. You know Bear Grylls, the adventurer and rugged outdoor type?

Bear launched a new TV show where men were challenged to survive on a desert island. They had to do macho and rugged tasks such as find food, shelter and drinking water. Most men I know these days would struggle to survive outdoors for less than half a day without phoning for a pizza.

Bear has suggested that masculinity in this country is in crisis, and he is right. He points out that modern man is too busy Facebooking or Tweeting. He is not, according to Bear, traditionally masculine any more.

There is, of course, nothing wrong with looking good, smelling nice and wearing decent clothes, but a line has now been crossed which sees a chap worshipping the pages of the latest male fashion magazine and turning themselves into some kind of hairless specimen no different from a mannequin you might see in a shop window.

Waxing (back, sack and crack) has taken male grooming to a new low. Men are supposed to be hairy, that is how they are built, but now you hear stories of blokes spending a fortune on laser hair-removal treatment because they want to be smooth. Oliver Reed would be turning in his grave.

Then there are these men who have an unhealthy obsession with television programmes such as *The Great British Bake Off* and *The Great British Sewing Bee*.

Real men can, of course, cook, but they do it for the love of food and to eat well, not because they want to turn up at work with a lighter than light sponge or to show off their piping bag skills to their colleagues. Proper men can also sew on a button, but should not be spending their time trying to make fancy tassels for a cushion they have just knocked up on a sewing machine.

For me, the day that signified the death of the real man was when that hideous sartorial creation the 'onesie' started to become perversely popular. Admittedly this garment is worn by both sexes, but no real man would wear one. Frankly, anyone sporting this silly garment should be ridiculed as an example to others.

For those who might be unfamiliar with this item, the onesie is a loose-fitting all-in-one jumpsuit-styled garment, usually made from fleecy material. High street stores, including John Lewis and Marks & Spencer, sell various ranges.

Of course the onesie is perfect if you are a child or an infant. Easy to put on, it requires little effort to clean and is quick to whip off and whack in the washing machine should you dribble your dinner down your front or have an accident because you could not make it to the loo in time. I have no problem with children or infants wearing onesies. A romper suit is about right on a two-year-old who has not quite mastered the art of eating and who still needs someone to wipe their bottom. Small children and onesies were meant to be. A fully grown male wearing one is downright peculiar.

Why would any self-respecting chap think that wearing a onesie would be a good idea? I have seen pictures circulating on social media of men who I know to be reasonably intelligent;

men with responsible jobs and of good character. And yet there they are, wearing their onesies
with pride. Several decades ago such behaviour
would have seen them banged up in the local
home for the bewildered — and quite rightly so.

Of course it is natural to unwind at the end
of the day and slip into something more com-
fortable that helps you relax, but to regress to
toddlerhood is pretty disturbing when you think
about it.

One can only imagine that when 'Pete' or
'Dave' hang up their suits after work and don
their onesies, they are going back to a time when
Mummy used to wind them after tea and they got
a lollipop and a bedtime story if they had been
good.

Tabloid newspapers used to make a fortune
when they published sensational stories about
celebrities or officials who paid money to a 'spe-
cialist lady' for services that included dressing
them up as babies and feeding them rusks. Now
it seems a variation of this behaviour is happening in living rooms up and down the land and

nobody is batting an eyelash. And you wonder why I mourn the death of the real man?

I will concede it can be tough being a fellow in the twenty-first century, particularly when it comes to what is right or wrong or deemed acceptable when dealing with members of the opposite sex. Any man with a brain should believe in equality; everyone should be treated equally regardless of their sex. This includes equal pay, the same career opportunities regardless of sex and the lifting of any restrictions enforced on the basis of gender. But I am helpless when it comes to defining what constitutes sexism these days and I doubt I am alone.

Pinching a woman's bottom, suggesting copulation in a lewd manner or marginalising a woman because of her sex are clearly forms of sexist behaviour, but there are many grey areas where a man can end up being branded a sexist and this is where my sympathy lies with the modern man.

Sadly I believe that there are a growing number of women who *look* for what they perceive to be sexist behaviour, and who are creating problems that do not exist. It can be a bloody and brutal minefield where just one or two words can cause offence and outrage.

As you may have already worked out, I have been at the sharp end of such an experience, which left me wondering if I really am some kind of sexist pig. I once worked in an office with a predominately female staff. My often cheery greeting when I arrived was an upbeat and heartfelt 'Hello, ladies', which I consider to be rather pleasant.

It appears not. I learned, to my astonishment, that such a remark can be interpreted to mean that I believe some women are ladies and others are not. Evidently I had made a distinction and judged one woman over another. Who knew? I was also accused of offering a greeting based on the gender of those I was talking to, which it was presumed I would never do to a group of men. I do not think any man worth his salt would ever consider this to be a form of sexist behaviour but, beware, for some women it can be.

The sisterhood operates in a warped way, just as it does when it condemns a man who calls a woman he may not know 'darling', 'sweetheart' or 'love'. There is no sexist intention, they are just everyday terms used right across Britain. Perceived sexism is a generational thing and from my experience it seems to be that younger women are the most likely to be offended. Genuine sexism, sadly, exists in society, but in order for it to be taken seriously and conquered, some rationality is required.

Aside from this sliver of sympathy towards the challenges confronting modern-day man, male generations coming through are letting the side down. Men do not seem to be men any more, instead they come across as weak and shallow individuals with no defined purpose or identity. The comedy duo 'The Two Ronnies' were way ahead of their time when they created a series of sketches for their programme entitled 'The Worm That Turned'.

Diana Dors guest-starred in this piece of dystopian fiction set in 2012 (though made in

1980) where women rule England. Male and female roles are totally reversed, even down to men having women's names and vice versa. Men are housekeepers and wear women's clothes, and law and order is managed by female guards in boots and hot pants.

The sketches can be found on YouTube and make for fun viewing and, while no one is suggesting that it represents our country now, I know plenty of men who would quite like to relinquish any responsibility in life as long as they were still allowed to watch *Top Gear* and play their video games.

In a last-ditch attempt to try to stop the rising tide of diminishing masculinity, I have put together a 'Real Man Manifesto' to help blokes struggling to define their maleness. I hope it helps and should leave men everywhere in no doubt as to the qualities that make a real man in the modern day.

Real men read maps; they do not rely on satnav. If you cannot read a map and reach a destination accordingly, then you really should not be behind the wheel of a vehicle. And, on the subject of driving, real men do not drive VW Beetles or the Fiat 500. These are, without question, cars for wimps.

Cooking and eating a large steak once a week is a sign of pure masculinity. Every man should know how to cook a steak, which should, of course, be eaten rare and bloody. Anything else suggests a removal of the taste buds.

Real men can also cook an omelette. If you have ever seen that fabulous film *The Ipcress File*, where Michael Caine plays spy Harry Palmer, you will know why. A perfect omelette speaks volumes and will impress any woman. It knocks a microwave meal for six.

To uphold the principles of pure masculinity, modern man should know how to catch, gut and clean a fish. He should be able to make a fire on the beach to cook it on.

Manners, the ability to make amusing small talk, capacity for seven pints of Guinness and the knack of changing a baby's nappy are also key to being a modern-day 'real' man. Failure to possess any of these key attributes will instantly have you sitting on the subs bench.

Real men refuse to participate in karaoke. They never play violent video games; they are *men*, not socially awkward teenagers.

Masculinity is in crisis and the real man is fast becoming an endangered species but it is still not too late to put masculinity back into Britain's menfolk. Meanwhile there are other, even more appalling trends on the rise, some of which may not be so easy to reverse — I am referring to the creation of and ever increasing obsession with celebrity culture.

8
I want to be a celebrity

I blame Jade Goody, Simon Cowell, Davina McCall and Michael Jackson. Each of them has played their own part in creating and fuelling our celebrity-obsessed culture. It is totally understandable too — there are millions of pounds to be made by satisfying a society that is so hooked on fame that it has long forgotten what really matters in life. There are hundreds of other names you could list too, but I think you get the general gist.

We have always had famous people or stars, but 'celebrity' is a recent phenomenon. How do you define it? As someone who is famous for five minutes or has become infamous as a result of something they have done in their personal life that only a few years ago would have seen them condemned outright and vilified. Now, if you want to make a quick quid and accelerate the process of attaining celebrity status you just need to sleep with a Premiership footballer or a pop star and you will make it onto the front page of the tabloids within moments.

Is this wrong? Who are we to judge? But

there is something pretty flawed in a society where such behaviour accords you the riches and rights that some people would kill for.

Simon Cowell is a genius of a man. He recognised very early on that people are becoming obsessed with fame and he created a couple of TV formats that not only tap in to this, but make vast amounts of money as well. *The X-Factor* and *Britain's Got Talent* are masterpieces in exploitation and tampering with the emotions of millions of viewers and everybody wins — the TV companies, the participants and the viewers. Advertising during these shows brings in serious cash, those that take part get their five minutes of fame and viewers across the country get to watch a programme that takes them on an emotional roller coaster. It even tells them when to cry or whoop with joy.

Big Brother is another programme that has taken people with no discernible talent and given them celebrity status. In the case of the late Jade Goody, it took someone who was not especially bright and, at times, a bit nasty, and turned them into someone famous for all the wrong reasons. What made the Goody story even more attractive to those obsessed with celebrity is that she died very prematurely at the age of twenty-seven from cervical cancer. It was like Princess Diana all over again, except without the baubles and conspiracy theories.

Davina McCall presented *Big Brother* for many years with a skill and insight the most experienced circus ringmaster would envy. But the most perverse thing about *Big Brother* is its celebrity version.

In order to further feed the hungry masses craving more celebrity content (and the same could be said for *I'm A Celebrity, Get Me Out Of Here!*), it took those people whose fame had slightly faded and gave them a second chance at the limelight. Entertainment agents around the country must have been rubbing their hands with glee at the prospect of making a few quid from the talent on their books who had spent the last several years doing pantomime in some obscure seaside town with no pier.

As a nation we lap it up and it show no signs of stopping. The world's obsession with Michael Jackson continues long after his death in a way that would make many cults envious. His death has created a billion-dollar business and presumably those that made a mint when he was alive are still profiteering from his talent long after his death.

The rise of celebrity seems to have cheapened fame. It is affecting children who, understandably, cannot see how contrived today's celebrity culture is and therefore want to be part of it.

A survey that compared the top career choices of 'then' and 'now' shows clearly how the aspirations of children have changed. The top three career choices of five- to eleven-year-olds in Britain today were sports star, pop star and actor, compared with teacher, banker and doctor thirty years ago. But if you cannot excel at a sport, sing or act, you can still make it big by demonstrating your low IQ, general ignorance or deeply unpleasant behaviour. Such behaviour used to be mocked, but now some catty woman, vicious old queen or dimwit gets lauded for being a 'character' and is anointed with 'celeb' status.

These people are so vapid and meaningless that they could never be called stars. However I suspect they are very happy with the celebrity 'tag' and the fact that they can sit in a roped-off area of a nightclub drinking cheap champagne just for turning up and giving the fame-obsessed punters a bit of a thrill on a Saturday night.

Our real stars are a dying breed. Roger Moore, Joan Collins, Helen Mirren, Michael Caine, Penelope Keith, Michael Ball, Sir Terry Wogan, Julie Walters and Paul O'Grady are all stars in my book, but I would struggle to double that list.

There are some that are hard to call. Hugh Grant, for example, should by rights be labelled a star, but his time in the spotlight over his various dalliances and his campaign against press intrusion have downgraded him to mere celebrity status, in my view.

The question of what defines star quality

is an interesting one. There clearly has to be genuine talent, but also a sense of one's own worth and perhaps knowing when to say no to something.

I also think that to be classed as a real star you have to keep something back that adds to the general intrigue about who you are and what you are going to do next. Our society now demands a constant supply of information and access to those that it deems famous which, if satisfied, only seems to erode star status.

Perhaps there are fewer stars about these days as 'show business' has been replaced by 'celebrity culture'. Let's be honest, anyone can become a celebrity, but you need talent and longevity to survive in show business and earn star status. These attributes seem to be in very short supply, but perhaps we only have ourselves to blame? Let's remember we are the nation who recently voted a dancing dog the winner of a television talent show where the prize was to perform in front of the Queen. She must have been so thrilled.

Modern-day Britain's focus on the latest celebrity birth or faux pas means the things that really matter, such as our identity and sense of place, get cast aside because they are a tad too challenging to think about.

9
Where am I?

Imagine you had no point of reference in terms of the place where you live. You had never been there before, yet you paid a visit for the first time. Would you know it was Ipswich, Truro, Colchester, Enfield, Southport, Cheltenham, Croydon, Huddersfield, Reading, Aberdeen, Barnstaple or any other place just by looking at the high street? I doubt it. If it were not for some notable landmarks, you could literally be anywhere in Britain. Our high streets have become clones of everywhere else around the country.

It is quite depressing. Get off a train or bus in any town or city and you will see the usual raft of high street names dotted all over the place. This is a symptom of a society driven by brands and a hunger for mass retail choice, but it has left many parts of Britain without a clear identity.

Coffee shops are a case in point. How many coffee shops does one town or high street need? They are all part of the same coffee chains, all serving the same product but just in a different style of packaging, with an image to suggest you are either supping an Americano from New York or an espresso made with the flavour of Italy by a barista who really comes from Clapham and whose name is Simon, not Luigi.

There are more and more shops being opened across Britain by national and worldwide brands, but, perversely, real choice is disappearing. This is particularly bad when you look at the restaurant scene. Britain's obsession with pizza and pasta is off the scale. There's quite a large collection of well-known high street names that satisfy the hunger of millions of customers every year, but a look at their menus clearly shows they are all knocking out plates of the same food that are no more than variations on a pretty limited theme.

The explosion of coffee shops and pseudo-Italian eateries of course creates jobs in an area and brings visitors, but it does nothing to support small, independent businesses who might fancy setting up a cafe or restaurant.

Rents and business rates are such that the bigger brand will always be able to locate and occupy a prime site compared to the small trader, and local councils seem to talk a good game about supporting the 'high street' but the reality seems very different.

According to the Centre for Retail Research, Britain now has 250,000 independent shops, compared with 750,000 in the mid-1960s. It has been predicted that a further 22 per cent of all stores, some 61,930 shops, will have gone by 2018.

The battle to save the high street has been lost. Many rail at the power of the supermarkets and our cloned high streets, but all of us have played a part in the changes. What incentive is there for a customer to remain loyal to a group of independent traders or a shop when they have to fork out for parking? You cannot blame people for choosing to save a few pounds by parking free of charge at the local supermarket. Once again you have to question the so-called commitment of local councils in promoting and preserving their high street when they frequently vote to introduce or increase parking charges in an area.

This lack of support, coupled with Britain's obsession with brands and high-street names and, of course, online shopping, will see the end of small traders and unique shops that give a place an identity. This is why, when you look about, you will increasingly see that everywhere looks the same.

Occasionally some government minister has the bright idea of using a name or a face to help save the high street. The most recent attempt was by retail guru Mary Portas, but it did not really work. It is one thing turning around a failing shop to provide material for a weekly television programme, it is something entirely different to do it in reality when the cameramen have disappeared and the stark realities of life as a small business are laid bare.

Some say the cloning of towns and streets is as a result of globalisation. It is affecting others too in a way that has never been seen before. The ongoing fight of London's black cab drivers is worth a mention here.

There are over 20,000 of these self-employed men and women who spend years and thousands of pounds gaining 'The Knowledge'.

London's black cabs are one of the most famous sights in the capital — they are iconic, and are on a level with red double-decker buses, Big Ben, Buckingham Palace and Trafalgar Square when it comes to sights that represent the city. It should come as no surprise that black cabs were used as part of one of the ceremonies to celebrate the London Olympics in 2012. They are representative of life in the capital.

The best way of describing 'The Knowledge' is to equate it to a mental atlas of London in your head. Those who have acquired it after years of study know the quickest run from one part of London to another. Hail a black cab at the kerb and they will take you the quickest route from a well-known landmark to a back street in north London, all without a satnav. To absorb all of these routes, many working to get their Green Badge spend years covering thousands of miles by scooter so they can take the test and pass 'The Knowledge'.

Understanding what black cab drivers have to go through to obtain the much-sought-after

Green Badge is important, as their livelihoods are under threat from rivals in the private hire and technology sectors who are desperate to pick up some of the business but without making the same commitment and sacrifices.

If the Mayor of London does not start to recognise the vital role the black cab community play in representing the capital, and if he does not introduce measures to protect their business, then we will see the slow demise of this world-famous trade and icon. London will just end up looking like any other city.

There is an old adage — sometimes you do not realise what you have got until it is gone. This has never been truer when it comes to protecting the identity of our streets, towns and cities.

The identity of places up and down Britain is being eroded at a worrying pace. To keep Britain unique and diverse, we really should be doing more to protect it. Instead, everyone seems to enjoy being spoon-fed a diet of blandness, buzzwords and uniformity, and no more so than in the modern workplace.

10
Working in hell

It is hard to believe but there was a time when life in the workplace was simple. You had a boss, you might have had a supervisor and you, with your colleagues, managed to rub along pretty effectively. There might have been the odd gripe or grumble but these were addressed by the man or woman in charge.

If you give people a clear structure of management and make them responsible and accountable, then they will get on with it and make a valued contribution to a business. Occasionally a member of staff might require a metaphorical kick up the backside, which could usually be achieved over an informal cup of coffee or early evening beer — but not any more.

The world of 'human resources', 'HR' and 'personnel' has grown massively over the last couple of decades and it is now a multi-billion-pound industry. It sustains thousands of consultants, hundreds of thousands of staff, conferences, seminars and a very buoyant publishing sector.

Modern-day business is obsessed with this world that seems to treat employees increasingly like morons. Nothing is guaranteed to annoy a workforce more than being patronised or talked down to by someone from HR. In my experience, those in human resources are perfectly well-meaning, but have read too many books by so-called HR gurus and have lost sight of how to deal with people in the real world.

Before earning a crust in the radio industry, I held down jobs in many different areas. I have worked in a warehouse loading and unloading lorries, in a bank, as a waiter and in a call centre. No matter what the sector, you were never too far away from having to appease almost militant diktats from the HR/personnel contingent.

Friends I talk to have experienced the same in their jobs. They often cite examples of how the HR department does not seem to exist to best support the employee, but actually to protect the management from discontent or to provide clever ways of controlling the workforce.

Many might think those in HR are their friends and the people to go to when you have a problem or grievance, but more often than not they are also the department responsible for rolling out training programmes or 'away days', which only seem to exist to ensure you toe the company line.

I have seen it first hand over the years and there has been an increase in organisations embracing an approach to staff management that is almost akin to brainwashing.

It is a clever yet highly Machiavellian method of running a company. I once worked for an organisation that kept preaching about their 'values-based' culture. These values supposedly centred on fairness, honesty and being professional, but the reality was the complete opposite when it came to those who were in charge. Hypocrisy would have been a mild charge to levy against them. I once witnessed a senior manager preaching about the importance of transparency in the workplace while ensuring that when it came to her own dealings with staff, there was no record or paper trail.

This incredibly false and disingenuous culture was effective when tackling staff who perhaps questioned the way the business was operated, but these so-called values were rarely used by the management themselves. This is a sure-fire way to breed resentment and distrust among workers.

More often than not, organisations that sub-scribe to this kind of management back up their ethos by running team-building or away days. I cannot believe I am alone in my animosity to such things. Many successful brands swear by them, rounding up their staff for some sort of annual weekend retreat that involves activities such as tree trekking and laser pigeon shoot-ing. In my experience, these outings are based around enforced participation, and often they only breed resentment. Wherever I have worked in the past, taking staff out for several beers and a curry can be the most effective form of team building. And it doesn't involve getting covered in mud either.

The trips I loathe are usually off-site and the activities organised by someone who makes a small fortune acting as a moderator or mentor.

These folk are curious people — it seems they have made a career out of playing such a role but, in my experience, they rarely have any solid experience of the real world. One person I came across claimed he had spent time with Native Americans as part of his life experience, which he thought best equipped him to lecture a workforce on how best to communicate with each other. His ego was the size of a house and I think he would have been better off playing alone with his very own totem pole.

Management and HR people do seem to talk in a different language compared to the rest of us. Words and phrases such as 'going forward', 'drilling down', 'competencies', 'stakeholders' and 'leverage' pepper conversations in a way that you would be forgiven for thinking was the symptom of some kind of Tourette's for those in middle-management.

The quality of managers these days has also taken a tumble. There was a time when being a good manager meant gaining the loyalty of your staff, possessing the backbone to make decisions and being prepared to go in to bat for those for whom you are responsible. These days 'successful' managers seem to rise to the top because of their ability to suck up to their superiors, shaft any of their staff at the drop of a hat and use words they are not entirely sure they understand in meetings.

Employees want a fair pay structure and appropriate rewards if the business achieves its targets. And saying 'thank you' every now and then means a hell of a lot more than endless appraisals and goal-setting or featuring someone in some highly patronising and divisive 'Employee of the Week' scheme. See, I told you, it really isn't that complicated.

But while workers may not feel fully appreciated by their companies, that is nothing compared to another travesty when it comes to how we deal with human beings in today's Britain. Over the last few years it has really come to light how badly we treat those in their twilight years. It is simply disgraceful.

11
Senior neglect

Our nation has been embarrassed — and rightly so — recently with reports of all kinds of incidents that show a distinct lack of respect for and understanding of our pensioners.

Repulsive video footage that was secretly filmed in care homes showed elderly and frail residents being verbally and physically abused. These victims were not murderers, criminals or prisoners of war — they were elderly ladies and gentlemen whose relatives mistakenly believed were being well looked after in a facility for which they were paying hundreds of pounds a week.

When these vile incidents of abuse come to light there is indignant outrage from the public, the perpetrators of the abuse are sacked and the care home in question issues an apology and that is it. Rarely are criminal charges brought against the individuals who carried out the abuse or the owners of the care home. Life goes on. You hope these cases are few and far between, but one cannot help but wonder if such abuse is more widespread, given that they only come to light thanks to secret cameras being placed by concerned family members or an investigative journalist. What about the unrecorded incidents?

Neglect of our elderly does not only happen in private institutions, but in the NHS too. I saw it first hand before my mother died in hospital after a complicated heart operation and several weeks of patchy care. The NHS faces many challenges in terms of resources and cash, but my gripe is the attitude I witnessed when it comes to treating those in their senior years.

There seems to be no understanding of the needs of an older person when in hospital. Someone in their seventies or eighties or older requires a bit more patience and explanation. Compared to younger patients, they are often more bewildered and scared of what is happening to them and just want someone to spend a bit more time and slowly explain what is going on. They also want to be able to ask questions without feeling they are a bit stupid or an irritant.

When visiting my mother in a number of NHS facilities, I was struck by how many of the nursing staff seem to consider older patients a bit of pain in the backside and witnessed many talking to such patients with borderline contempt. I accept being an overworked and stressed-out nurse would try the patience of a saint, but that is no excuse for treating an elderly patient like a dumb and wretched animal.

It was also very clear to me that, generally, nurses and medical staff from overseas seemed to have a greater respect and understanding of the needs of elderly patients compared to British employees. I think we could learn a thing or two from how other countries treat their elderly relatives and citizens.

The government also seems hell-bent on making things as difficult as possible for Britain's elderly population. One idea which has been floated was to make more government services only accessible via the Internet. This included the Carer's Allowance. Office of National Statistics figures reveal that there are around four million homes without Internet access in Britain — many of those are lived in by citizens in their senior years. Technology has left some aged sixty-five or over isolated. A recent report by a think-tank estimated that four out of ten people over sixty-five did not have access to the Internet at home, with more than five million saying they had never been online.

Those who do not want to go online would be offered a one-off lesson to teach them the joys of the Internet and then that would be that. But no thought seems to have been given to how a senior citizen would be able to afford their own computer or broadband if they are surviving on a tight budget or pension.

In a country where we still hear of shameful stories of some OAPs having to choose between eating or heating in the winter months, such a scheme to make more of the state's services 'online-only' is at best insensitive and, at worst, cruel. Politicians say it is about saving the country money, but you have to ask at what cost?

Neglect takes many forms and it is not just

about care and our attitude towards pensioners we should be concerned about, it is satisfying future demands as our senior population increases in size and lives for longer. Successive governments have failed to grasp this, but the figures speak for themselves. We are in serious danger of leaving millions of OAPs in this country without the resources, care and support they all deserve in their later years.

Figures from the charity Age UK show how our country is changing at a pace unmatched by government and political action. There will soon be a large proportion of the population significantly over the age of sixty-five and little is being done to prepare for this time.

There are currently 10.8 million people aged sixty-five or over in the UK. There are now more people in the UK aged sixty and above than there are under eighteen and more pensioners than children under sixteen. Predictions for the future make it abundantly clear. The number of people aged sixty or over is expected to pass twenty million by 2031. The amount of people over eighty-five is predicted to double in the next twenty years and almost treble in the next thirty.

Dementia, of course, is also an issue with a growing elderly population. In 2012 the Alzheimer's Society released figures showing that there were 800,000 people in Britain with dementia. This figure is projected to increase to one million by 2021 and 1.7 million in 2051.

Economists have written at length about Britain's predicted pension crisis and there is a perfect combination of factors that will contribute to a problem that could leave many vulnerable in their twilight years. The approach from the majority of our politicians appears to be increasing the age that the state pension is payable from and encouraging us to save more.

But many people are simply unable to save more than they already are. Continually raising the retirement age does little to address the cause of the crisis.

The sums are simple enough. Take the Age UK figures and, bar an explosion in people procreating, we will not have a sufficient working population paying enough tax to fund the pension requirements of our large and increasing elderly population in decades to come.

Isolation, the growth in dementia, a deficit in pensions and an increasing pressure on health and social care are all challenges which a growing senior population will generate. While all of this neglect might not be felt at this moment, it is a ticking time bomb and one that makes me quite frightened of becoming a senior citizen.

Charities do an amazing job in caring and providing support for Britain's senior population, but they can only continue to do so much. Our attitude in Britain needs to change drastically if we are going to return to a time when our elderly population was treated with reverence, decency and respect. Our government needs to face up to the challenge of ensuring enough funding is available to meet the practical requirements and the rest of us need to stop treating our seniors as some kind of irritating burden.

Conclusion

The last twenty-plus years have not been kind to Britain and our society has become more insular, selfish, unquestioning and ignorant than ever before. I love this country, but this does not mean blind allegiance without criticism or questioning. Sadly, apathy is so rife we appear to lack the balls or energy to do much about it.

Such an attitude would never be tolerated in France. Whatever you think of the French, they have an enviable track record of taking to the streets and standing up for what they believe in. They are politically and socially engaged, treat 'fluffiness' with the contempt it deserves and generally seem to care a lot more about the stuff that matters. They also have the highest regard for their elders. Perhaps we should adopt the French approach to life instead of stewing in a dumbed-down froth of ignorance, fakery and mediocrity. Mind you, the French have not got it right with their smoking ban either, but I hear that it is rarely enforced in the same zealous way that it is in Britain.

Not voting; technology replacing verbal communication; the smoking ban; the depressing lack of food knowledge; the rise of the NIMBY; the inability to debate; celebrity culture; the cloning of our towns and cities; the demise of the real man; the amount of guff we put up with in the workplace; and how appallingly we treat our senior citizens are all areas that I believe have contributed to a new supersized, dumbed-down Britain. Could it change? Yes, if the real desire is there, but it will take time. Perhaps secretly many enjoy the comatose and unchallenging state they find themselves in. A look at the future does not bode well for those of you that have enjoyed this book. Driverless cars, meal replacement drinks and living in a world increasingly dominated by simulated experiences are all likely to hack off those of us who crave more from life. It is enough to drive you to strong drink. You'd better make mine a large one...cheers!

About LBC

LBC is Britain's only national news talk radio station. It tackles the big issues of the day, with intelligent, informed and provocative opinion from guests, listeners and presenters, including Nick Ferrari, James O'Brien, Shelagh Fogarty, Iain Dale, Ken Livingstone, David Mellor and Beverley Turner. LBC reaches 1.2 million people in Britain and is available on DAB digital radio, online at lbc.co.uk, through mobile apps, Sky Digital Channel 0112, Virgin Media Channel 919 and on 97.3FM in London.

About the Series

In this major new series, popular LBC presenters tackle the big issues in politics, current affairs and society. We might applaud their views; we might be outraged. But these short, sharp polemics are destined to generate controversy, discussion and debate — and lead Britain's conversation.

Titles in the series

Steve Allen, *So You Want to Be a Celebrity?*
Duncan Barkes, *The Dumbing Down of Britain*
Iain Dale, *The NHS: Things That Need to Be Said*
Nick Ferrari, *It's Politics … But Not As We Know It*
James O'Brien, *Loathe Thy Neighbour*